PEAK DISTRICT Eﬀ

BY

JOHN N. MERRILL

MAPS AND PHOTOGRAPHS

BY JOHN N. MERRILL

a J.N.M. PUBLICATION

1988

a J.N.M. PUBLICATION

JNM PUBLICATIONS,
WINSTER,
MATLOCK,
DERBYSHIRE.
DE4 2DQ

Conceived, edited, typeset, designed, marketed and distributed by John N. Merrill.

© Text and routes — John N. Merrill 1986 and 1988

© Maps and photographs — John N. Merrill 1988

First Published — October 1986.
This edition — April 1988.

ISBN 0 907496 39 3

Meticulous research has been undertaken to ensure that this publication is highly accurate at the time of going to press. The publishers, however, cannot be held responsible for alterations, errors or omissions, but they would welcome notification of such for future editions.

Printed by: Linprint, Mansfield, Nottinghamshire.

ABOUT JOHN N. MERRILL

John combines the characteristics and strength of a mountain climber with the stamina, and athletic capabilities of a marathon runner. In this respect he is unique and has to his credit a whole string of remarkable long walks. He is without question the world's leading marathon walker.

Over the last ten years he has walked more than 55,000 miles and successfully completed ten walks of at least 1,000 miles or more.

His six walks in Britain are—

Hebridean Journey	1,003 miles
Northern Isles Journey	913 miles
Irish Island Journey	1,578 miles
Parkland Journey	2,043 miles
Lands End to John O'Groats	1,608 miles

and in 1978 he became the first person (permanent Guinness Book Of Records entry) to walk the entire coastline of Britain—6,824 miles in ten months.

In Europe he has walked across Austria (712 miles), hiked the Tour of Mont Blanc and GR20 in Corsica as training! In 1982 he walked across Europe—2,806 miles in 107 days—crossing seven countries, the Swiss and French Alps and the complete Pyrennean chain—the hardest and longest mountain walk in Europe.

In America he used the world's longest footpath—The Appalachian Trail (2,200 miles) as a training walk. The following year he walked from Mexico to Canada in record time—118 days for 2,700 miles.

During the summer of 1984, John set off from Virginia Beach on the Atlantic coast, and walked 4,226 miles without a rest day, across the width of America to San Francisco and the Pacific Ocean. This walk is unquestionably his greatest achievement, being, in modern history, the longest, hardest crossing of the USA in the shortest time—under six months (177 days). The direct distance is 2,800 miles.

Between major walks John is out training in his own area —the Peak District National Park. As well as walking in other areas of Britain and in Europe he has been trekking in the Himalayas four times. He lectures extensively and is author of more than sixty books.

CONTENTS

INTRODUCTION

I am often asked, 'what is your favourite walk in the Peak District?' With such variety of walking in such a small area, it is a hard question to answer. But, in the final analysis I resort to the two walks I first did when I was 'a wee young lad'! The first was along the gritstone edges—a walk I have done more than forty times! The other is down the limestone dales—this I have walked more than thirty times! These two walks make ideal 'bashes' or 'flogs' and can be knocked off in about eight hours each. But I am flippant, for they are the grandslam of Peak District beauty and always a joy to walk.

The gritstone edge route has for me become an annual event; usually New Year's Day. I set off carrying a bottle of whisky, a chicken leg and a large hunk of Christmas cake. My rules are simple—walk end to end, do a climb on each edge as I go, and have a drink on every edge! Generally I do hard climbs first, but as the walk progresses and the effort and alchohol take effect, the climbs become easier and easier. I know of no finer 'first footing' and each year I look forward to yet another epic. News of my walks has got around and more recently there have been 'Merrill watchers' on the various edges. To add to the spice of the annual struggle I have taken to wearing a disguise and sometimes fancy dress to confuse the 'spies', looking for a bearded, tottering shorts-wearing walker!

The limestone dale route is a summer walk for me in June when the flowers are at their best and many dales full of orchids. Apart from the Dovedale/Wolfscote Dale section, I rarely meet anyone and enjoy the solitude of a long day's hike. I carry no liquid and have a couple of bars of chocolate to sustain me. My June 1986 walk was full of superlatives, being crystal clear weather and 80 degrees, leaving me burnt and rather red on reaching Ashbourne, but five pounds lighter in weight!

Here then are my two favourite long walks in the Peak District. I never tire of walking them and hope you too come to love them and walk them often. Both, as you head north to south, are basically downhill! Have a good walk and let me know how you get on. Perhaps I will see you? In the dales, look for a guy in shorts devouring chocolate, and on the edges keep your eye open for a bottle swigging climber wearing a wig!

Happy walking!

John N. Merill.

JOHN N. MERRILL

Since 1986 more than 700 people have walked one or both the routes; some wearing wigs!

1

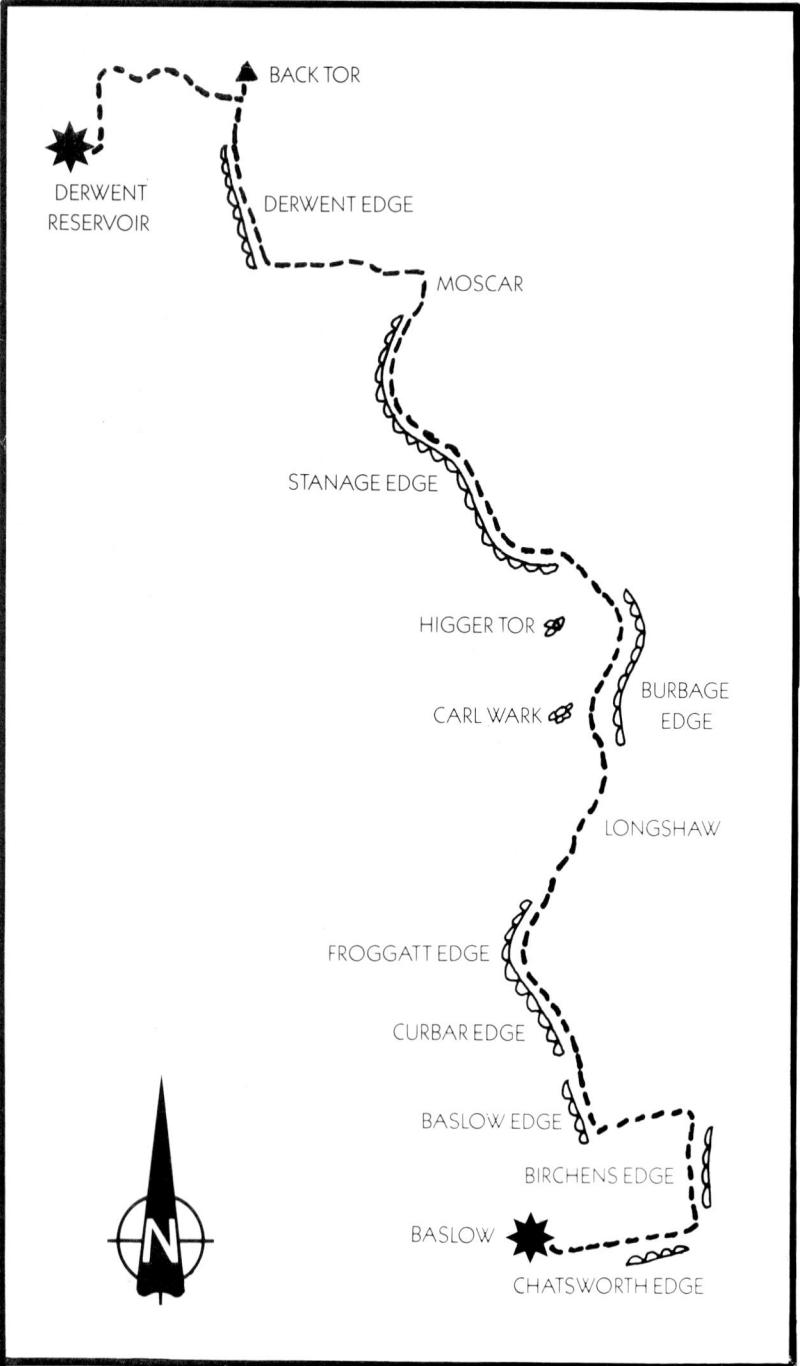

BACK TOR

DERWENT RESERVOIR

DERWENT EDGE

MOSCAR

STANAGE EDGE

HIGGER TOR

CARL WARK

BURBAGE EDGE

LONGSHAW

FROGGATT EDGE

CURBAR EDGE

BASLOW EDGE

BIRCHENS EDGE

BASLOW

CHATSWORTH EDGE

N

THE GRITSTONE EDGE WALK—
23 MILES—allow 8-10 hours

ABOUT THE WALK—

The walk is devised to be done in a single day with your wife, girlfriend or support party dropping you off at Fairholmes car park. The first three miles are the hardest as you ascend to Back Tor. From there, as you head southwards you are basically heading downhill with a few brief ascents. The route is broken down into stages where support parties can meet you to attend to blisters and give you the incentive to push on! There are vertually no amenities along the route, apart from two inns that you pass, more than half way along the route. A third—Fox House Inn—lies just off the route. Baslow, the end, has everything!

At the Burbage Valley with there being several paths you can select which one—either down the valley, along the top of the edge or over Higger Tor and Carl Wark. Upon reaching Wellington's Monument at the end of Baslow Edge, there is an easy way straight down to Baslow, but this is frowned upon for there are three more edges to go! For those who complete the walk a special four colour embroidered badge on a brown (Gritstone) background and a completion certificate is available from JNM Publications. A master record of all who walk the route is maintained by me.

The whole route is covered by the Ordnance Survey maps

1:25,000—Outdoor Leisure map—The Dark Peak
1:25,000—Pathfinder Series—Sheet No SK28/38—Sheffield
1:25,000—Outdoor Leisure Map—The White Peak (East Sheet)

GEOLOGY NOTES—The Peak District is principally made up of two different types of rock belonging to the Carboniferous System—gritstone and limestone. The rock's strata is saucer shaped resulting from earth movement. This exposed the softer gritstone which over the millions of years has worn away exposing the harder and more durable limestone. The rock formation is often called the 'Derbyshire Dome.' It is for this reason there is a large limestone plateau with numerous dales which is surrounded on three sides by the gritstone outcrops. The gritstone, known as the Millstone Grit series is a useful building material and along the edges was extensively used for millstones; many can still be seen lying around.

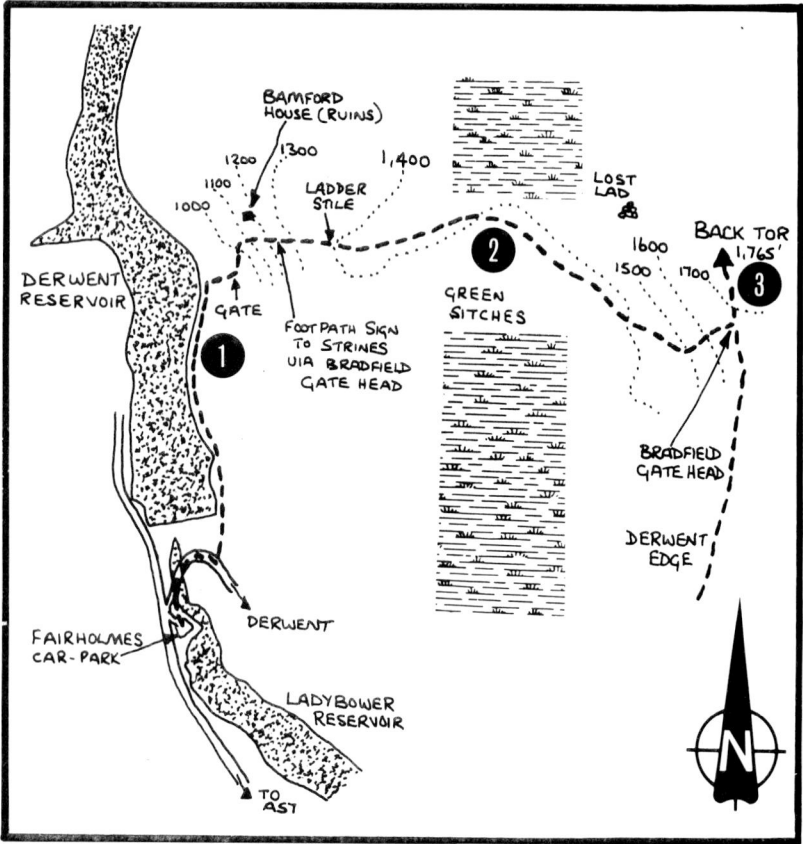

BAMFORD HOUSE (RUINS)

1300

1200

1100

1000

1,400

LADDER STILE

LOST LAD

BACK TOR 1,765'

1600

1500   1700

DERWENT RESERVOIR

GATE

FOOTPATH SIGN TO STRINES VIA BRADFIELD GATE HEAD

GREEN SITCHES

BRADFIELD GATE HEAD

DERWENT EDGE

FAIRHOLMES CAR-PARK

DERWENT

LADYBOWER RESERVOIR

TO A57

N

DERWENT RESERVOIR

4

FAIRHOLMES TO BACK TOR—
3 MILES & 1,000 feet of ascent

ABOUT THE SECTION—

First you walk beside Derwent Reservoir before ascending, steeply at first, through moorland to Derwent Edge and Back Tor's summit. Although just to the left of the route, the summit is a magnificent vantage point.

MAP—*1:25,000 Outdoor Leisure Map — The Dark Peak.*

WALKING INSTRUCTIONS—

From the car-park walk past the toilets and Information Office on your left and gain the path through woodland to the road. Bear right along it as it curves right with the dam wall of Derwent Reservoir on your left. Follow it round to a path on your left; here leave the road and head northwards through the trees to the stile close to the dam wall. Continue ahead on a wide track with the reservoir on your left. Follow it for just over ½ mile to the aptly named Walker's Clough on your right. Turn right and ascend the path with a stream on your right to a gate. Continue on a defined path as you ascend steeply first to your right, then left to a wall and stream. Here the path bears right as you continue ascending to a metal footpath sign—Strines via Bradfield Gate.

Here the angle eases as you continue on the path to a ladder stile. Over this you follow a track for about ¼ mile before leaving it on your right as you cross the moorland of Green Sitches and ascend to Bradfield Gate Head. The path can be seen from the ladder stile. Pass two footpath signs stating—Abney Grange and Strines. On the top, close to Derwent Edge on your right, gain the path which will lead along the edge and southwards. Before doing so the triangulation pillar on Back Tor is on your left and worth the few extra strides to gain the gritstone outcrop and its extensive view.

LADYBOWER RESERVOIR—The last reservoir in the Derwent Valley scheme to be built in 1945. Howden Reservoir at the head of the valley was completed in 1912 and has a holding capacity of 1,980 million gallons. Derwent Reservoir was completed in 1912 and has a capacity of 2,120 million gallons. Ladybower is the largest with a capacity of 6,310 million gallons.

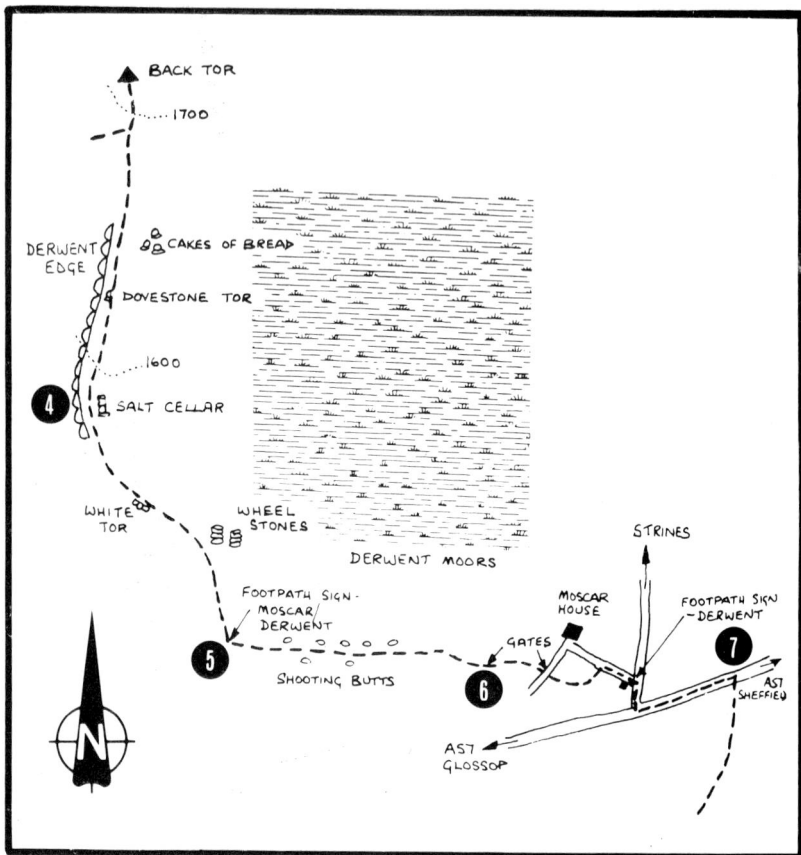

BACK TOR

1700

DERWENT EDGE

CAKES OF BREAD

DOVESTONE TOR

1600

4 SALT CELLAR

DERWENT MOORS

WHITE TOR

WHEEL STONES

STRINES

FOOTPATH SIGN - MOSCAR / DERWENT

MOSCAR HOUSE

FOOTPATH SIGN - DERWENT

5

7

GATES

6

SHOOTING BUTTS

A57 SHEFFIELD

A57 GLOSSOP

N

WHEEL STONES

6

BACK TOR TO MOSCAR—4 MILES

ABOUT THE SECTION-

Descending all the way past a variety of rock formations—Cakes of Bread, Salt Cellar and Wheel Stones! Magnificent views and my favourite slice of the walk!

MAPS—*1:25,000 Outdoor Leisure Map—The Dark Peak—1:25,000 Pathfinder Series—Sheet No SK28/38—Sheffield*

WALKING INSTRUCTIONS—

Retrace your steps back to Bradfield Gate Head and continue ahead on the path with Derwent Edge on your right. Shortly you pass the Cakes of Bread on your left before reaching Dovestone Tor. Continue on to pass close to the Salt Cellar on your right before gaining White Tor a little over ¼ mile later—just after you walk off the Dark Peak map. Keep to the well defined path to the next rock formation—Wheel Stones. ⅓ mile later reach the footpath junction and path sign—Moscar/Derwent. Here turn left and begin descending past numerous grouse shooting butts. A mile later pass through a gate and follow a track to another gate beside another path sign—Via Derwent Edge to Derwent. Cross the walled track to Moscar House and keep the wall on your left as you follow the path around it to another track, beside a footpath sign. Turn right up the track, through a gate and past a house on your right before reaching the Strines road and Derwent path sign. Turn right to A57 road and turn left to walk beside for ¾ mile to the footpath sign and stile on your right, for Stanage Edge.

SALT CELLAR

7

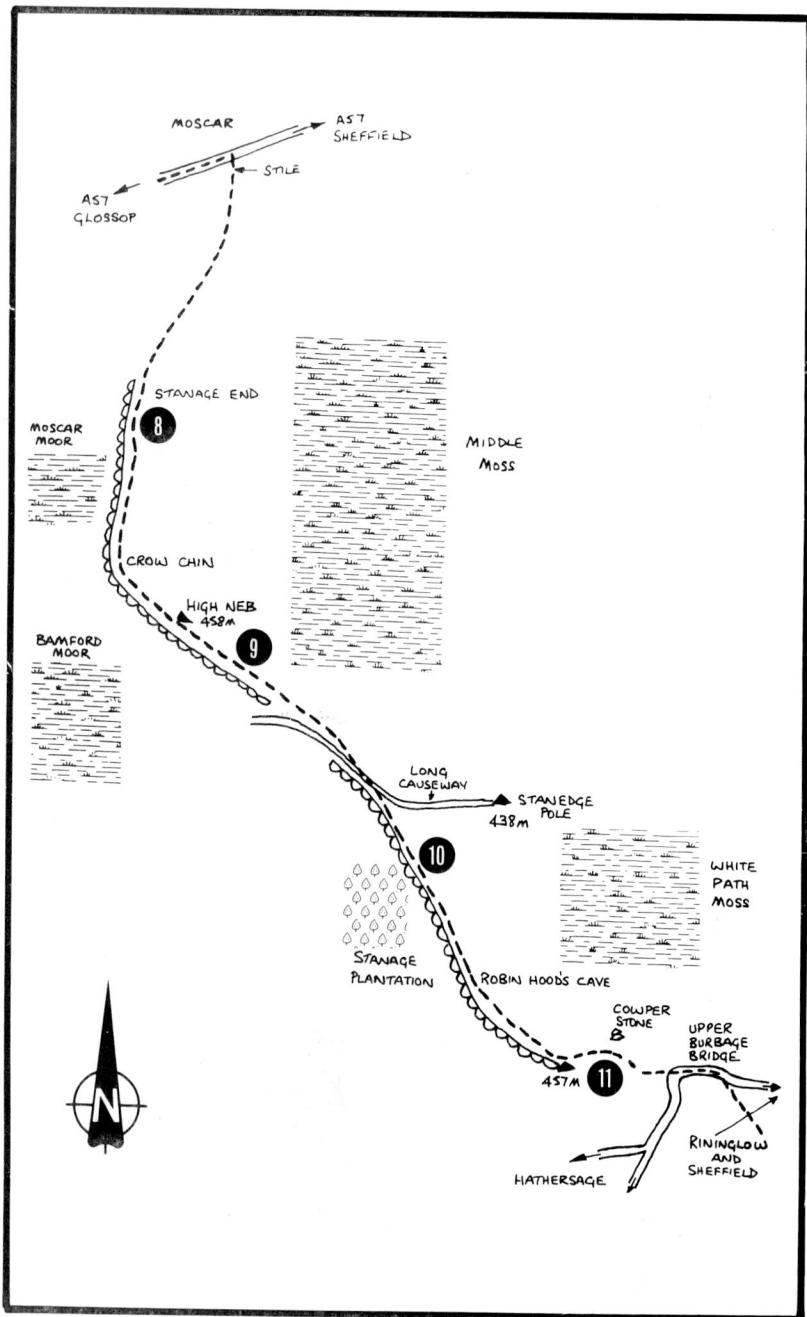

MOSCAR

A57 SHEFFIELD

A57 GLOSSOP

STILE

STANAGE END

8

MOSCAR MOOR

MIDDLE MOSS

CROW CHIN

HIGH NEB 458M

9

BAMFORD MOOR

LONG CAUSEWAY

STANEDGE POLE 438M

10

WHITE PATH MOSS

STANAGE PLANTATION

ROBIN HOOD'S CAVE

COWPER STONE

UPPER BURBAGE BRIDGE

457M

11

N

HATHERSAGE

RINGINGLOW AND SHEFFIELD

MOSCAR TO BURBAGE BRIDGE—4½ MILES

ABOUT THE SECTION—

A short but gradual ascent brings you onto Stanage Edge, the longest gritstone edge in the Peak District, with more than 600 climbs. A favourite whisky halt of mine is Robin Hood's Cave!

MAP—*1:25,000 Pathfinder Series—Sheet No SK28/38—Sheffield*

WALKING INSTRUCTIONS—

Leave the A57 opposite Moscar Lodge, and ascend the stile beside the footpath sign. The first mile you ascend about 300 feet along a well defined path/track to Stanage End. Just as you reach here and the remains of a small quarry, bear left onto the crest of the edge. There is a path beneath the edge if you prefer. Continue along the top of the edge heading for the cairns at Crow Chin before the triangulation pillar on High Neb. The path is well used as you press on to a ladder stile and gain the Long Causeway track from Stanedge Pole. Follow it briefly before continuing ahead, at the Open Country sign, along the top of Stanage Edge. Beneath you are the trees of Stanage Plantation and a ¼ mile later Robin Hood's Cave. You are now walking along the best part of the edge heading for the next triangulation pillar at the southern end of Stanage Edge. The actual pillar lies just to your right off the main pathline. Here the path turns left and descends with the Cowper Stone on your left as you descend to the road close to Upper Burbage Bridge and the Ringinglow/Sheffield road.

STANAGE EDGE

9

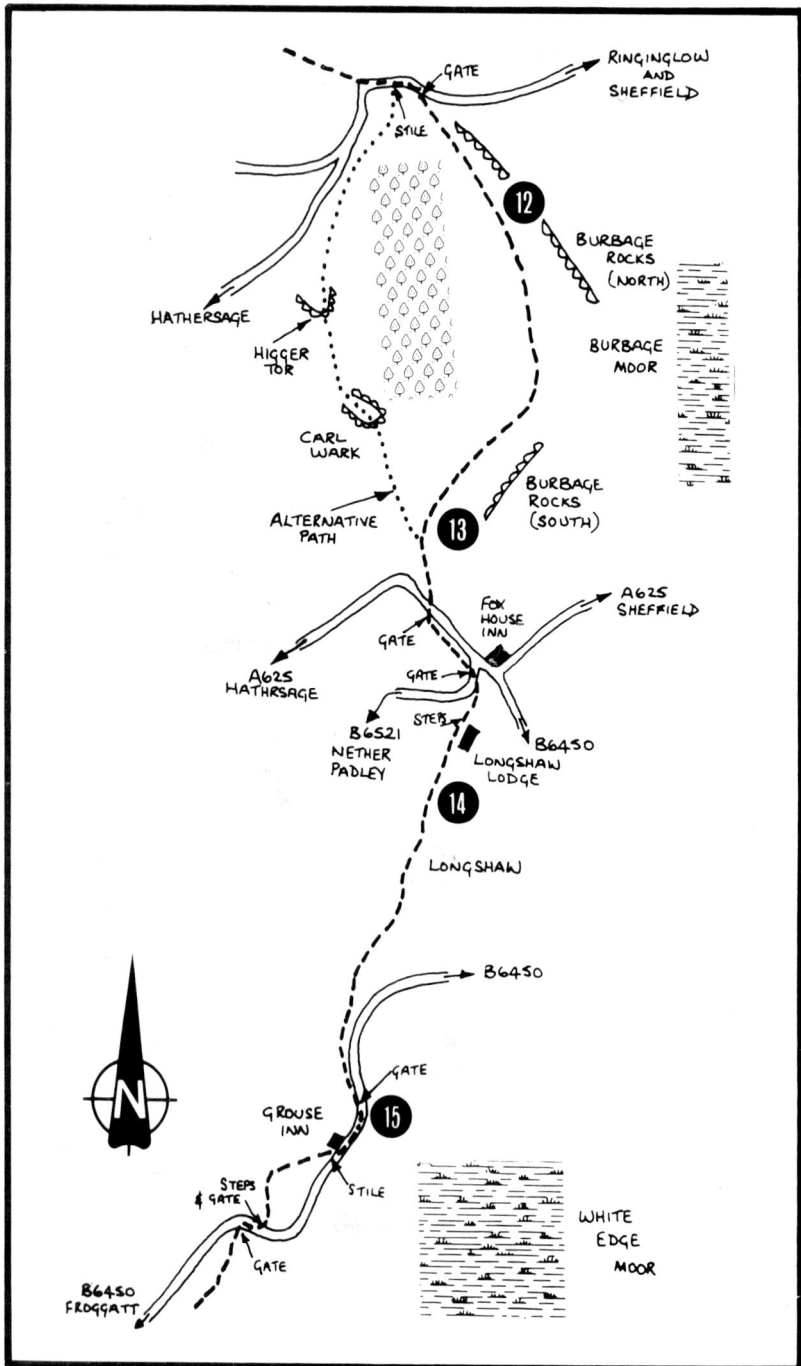

GATE

RINGINGLOW
AND
SHEFFIELD

STILE

12

BURBAGE
ROCKS
(NORTH)

HATHERSAGE

HIGGER
TOR

BURBAGE
MOOR

CARL
WARK

BURBAGE
ROCKS
(SOUTH)

ALTERNATIVE
PATH

13

FOX
HOUSE
INN

A625
SHEFFIELD

GATE

A625
HATHRSAGE

GATE

STEPS

B6521
NETHER
PADLEY

B6450

LONGSHAW
LODGE

14

LONGSHAW

B6450

GATE

GROUSE
INN

15

N

STEPS
& GATE

STILE

GATE

WHITE
EDGE
MOOR

B6450
FROGGATT

BURBAGE TO FROGGATT—4 MILES

ABOUT THE SECTION—

Descending all the way with a choice of routes in the Burbage Valley — either along the valley floor, over Higger Tor and Carl Wark or along the crest of the Burbage Edge. All three have well defined paths and here I describe the 'traditional' route along the valley floor. At the end of the valley at the A625—Sheffield-Hathersage road—there is the Fox House Inn just up the road to your left. In Longshaw there is a cafe and close to Froggatt is the Grouse Inn, which you walk past! Longshaw serves as a delightful interlude between the edge country as you walk through pleasant woodland.

MAPS—*1:25,000 Pathfinder Series—*
Sheet No SK28/38—Sheffield—1:25,000 Outdoor Leisure Map—
The White Peak (East Sheet)

WALKING INSTRUCTIONS—

Go through the gated stile beside the car park at Upper Burbage Bridge and begin descending the track through the valley past the rocks of Burbage north on your left. Still a favourite climbing ground of mine and one of the few edges that I have climbed in total! Keep on the track for two miles to the A625 road. The Higger Tor and edge crest routes all join the valley path at the southern end.

Cross the A625 road to a footpath gate and enter Longshaw, National Trust property. The path soon turns left as you ascend gently to the B6521 road (Grindleford). Cross the road and enter Longshaw along the driveway. Here you walk onto the White Peak map. On approaching the buildings of Longshaw Lodge, with the cafe and Information Centre on your left, descend the steps and follow the path round to a gate. Beyond go through another and follow the grass driveway through Longshaw Country Park. Keep on it to the B6054 road (Froggatt) a mile away. Turn right and walk beside the road to the Grouse Inn. Just beyond it is the stile and path across the fields to the car park. Here turn left, as footpath signed and descend to a small stream before ascending the steps to the B6054 road. Opposite to your right is the start of the Froggatt Edge path.

LONGSHAW—a former shooting lodge and estate of the Duke of Rutland; owners of Haddon Hall. Today the lodge and estate is owned by the National Trust who have an Information Centre and tea room here.

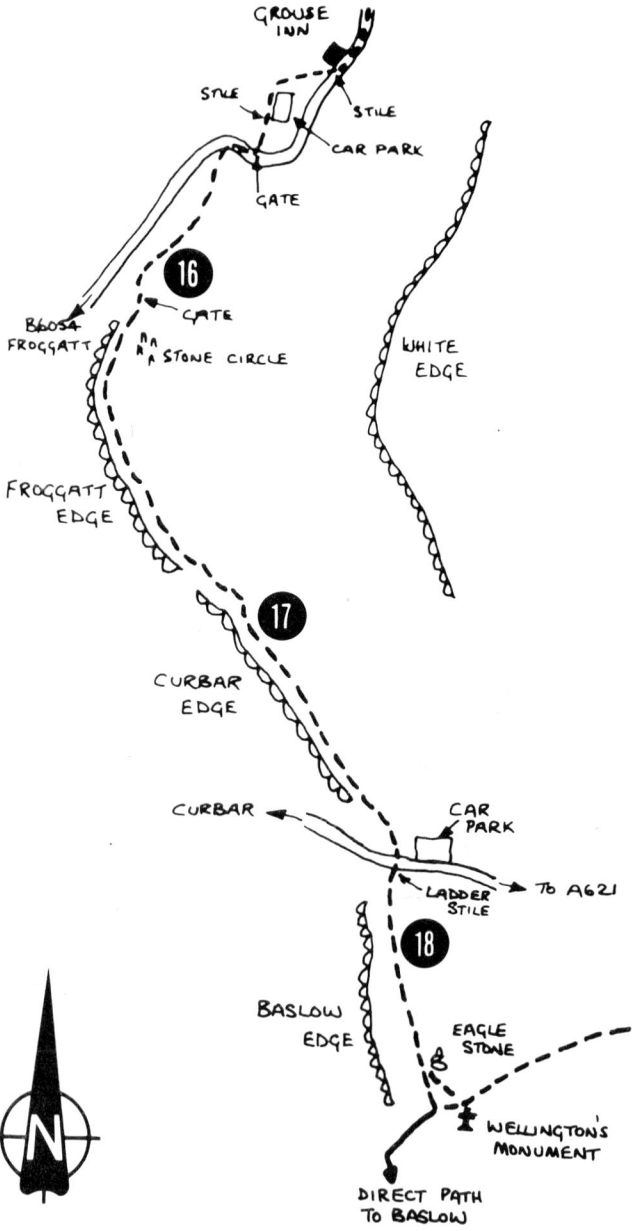

GROUSE INN

STILE

STILE

CAR PARK

GATE

16

B6054 FROGGATT

GATE

STONE CIRCLE

WHITE EDGE

FROGGATT EDGE

17

CURBAR EDGE

CURBAR

CAR PARK

To A621

LADDER STILE

18

BASLOW EDGE

EAGLE STONE

WELLINGTON'S MONUMENT

DIRECT PATH TO BASLOW

N

FROGGATT TO
WELLINGTON'S MONUMENT—3 MILES

ABOUT THE SECTION—

Apart from a slight ascent on Froggatt Edge you are descending all the way along the top of some of the most spectacular edges in the Peak District, with Curbar Edge being one of the highest natural gritstone faces full of hard climbs. Close to Wellington's Monument is the Eagle Stone—a nice challenging boulder problem!

MAP—*1:25,000 Outdoor Leisure Map — The White Peak (East Sheet)*

WALKING INSTRUCTIONS—

Leave the B6054 road and follow the track onto Froggatt Edge, first passing through woodland. The path is well defined and the edge is nearby for a saunter to watch climbers on a route or to see the Froggatt Pinnacle. Three miles along here and you descend to the minor road and nearby car park at Curbar Gap. Cross the road and ascend the ladder stile and continue along the track with Baslow Edge far to your right. Ahead can be seen the Eagle Stone and Wellington's Monument ½ mile away.

EAGLE STONE—said to be named after the god, Aigle, who could lift boulders that other couldn't! The stone is also known as a Lover's Stone. Before a local couple could get married the man had to prove himself by climbing the rock. If you didn't get to the top—no marriage!

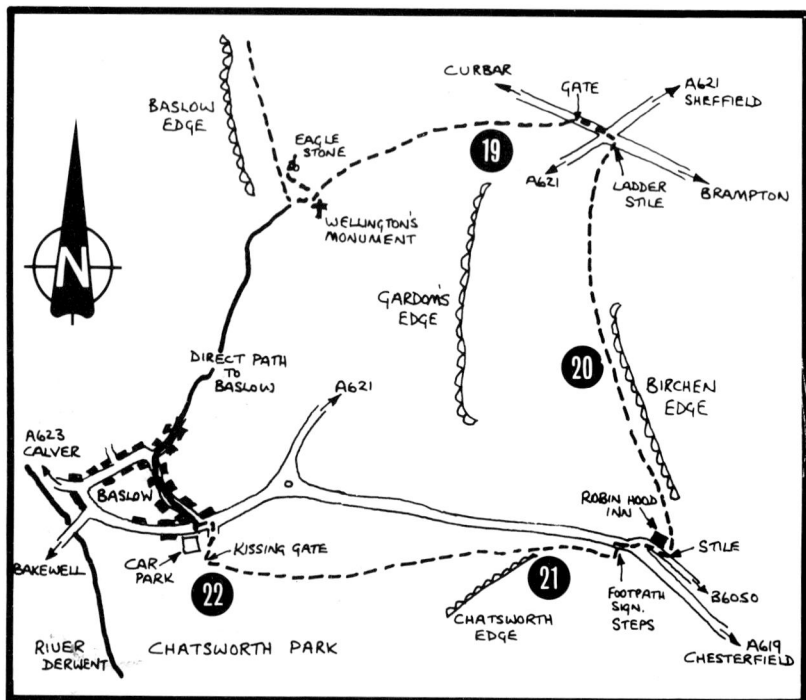

BASLOW EDGE

EAGLE STONE

CURBAR

GATE

A621 SHEFFIELD

A621

LADDER STILE

BRAMPTON

19

WELLINGTON'S MONUMENT

GARDOM'S EDGE

20

BIRCHEN EDGE

DIRECT PATH TO BASLOW

A621

A623 CALVER

BASLOW

ROBIN HOOD INN

STILE

BAKEWELL

CAR PARK

KISSING GATE

22

CHATSWORTH EDGE

21

FOOTPATH SIGN. STEPS

B6050

A619 CHESTERFIELD

RIVER DERWENT

CHATSWORTH PARK

WELLINGTON'S MONUMENT—records the visit of the Iron Duke who died in 1852.

NELSON'S MONUMENT—erected in 1810 by John Brightman of Baslow. Close by are three shiplike stones bearing the names, Victory, Defiant and Royal.

WELLINGTON'S MONUMENT
TO BASLOW—4 MILES

ABOUT THE SECTION—

Slightly cruel after such a long walk to see Baslow one mile away, but your route is four more. The view from the monument is impressive and it would be a shame to miss Birchens and Chatsworth Edges, especially as you walk past the Robin Hood Inn! Complete this section and you have earned a hot bath and a succulent steak with mushrooms!

MAP—*1:25,000 Outdoor Leisure Map—The White Peak (East Sheet)*

WALKING INSTRUCTIONS—

Turn left at the monument along the track, heading eastwards to the minor road to Curbar ½ mile away. Turn right and cross the A621 Baslow road onto the Brampton Road, and turn right over the ladder stile into Open Country. The path is well defined, ascending slightly to the base of Birchens Edge. To your right is Gardoms Edge. Follow the path beneath the edge and no doubt watch a climber ascending one of the many routes. It is a great place to learn here and not too far to fall off! The path descends through silver birch trees to a stile well to the left of the car park and Robin Hoods Inn. Turn right past the inn to the A619 Chesterfield road. Turn right and left almost immediately, across the road to the concessionary path through Chatsworth Park to Baslow, 1½ miles away.

First descend the steps and cross the stream before bearing right to a track which you follow passing your last edge, Chatsworth Edge on your left. Enter Chatsworth Park via an extremely high stone stile. The final mile is now at hand as you descend the grass of the Park; keep to the righthand side of the Park and after ¾ mile gain the main footpath to Chatsworth House, beside the tall metal kissing gate. Turn right through it and follow the track round to Bar Brook and into the Nether End side of Baslow with its car park, cafe, shop, inns and steak house. What more can you ask for after such an enthralling walk down some of the Peak District's finest scenery?

BAR BROOK, BASLOW—the thatched cottage here is linked to a macabre story which happened 200 years ago. A tramp called at the cottage and forcibly obtained food from the owner. He became so enraged that he grabbed a pan of hot fat and poured it down her throat, killing her. He was caught three days later and was sentenced to be gibbetted alive in chains. His screams could be heard for miles and the Duke of Devonshire ensured this was the last live gibbet in Derbyshire.

PLACE	TELEPHONE	TOILET	CAR PARK	POST OFFICE	SHOP	RESTAURANT	INN	CAMPING	YHA	B & B
FAIRHOLMES	●	●						●		
A57		●								
LONGSHAW	●	●		●			●			
FROGGATT		●					●			
BIRCHENS			●				●	●		
BASLOW	●	●	●	●	●	●	●			●

There are very few amenities actually on the route until Baslow where there is everything.

INNS—on or very close to route

Fox House Inn,	Longshaw—200 yards from route
Grouse Inn,	near Froggatt Edge
Robin Hood Inn,	near Birchens Edge
The Devonshire Arms,	Baslow
Wheatsheaf Hotel,	Baslow

YOUTH HOSTEL

Hagg Farm —
1½ miles from start of route.
Tel. Hope Valley (0433) 51594
National Park hostel managed by the Peak
Park Joint Planning Board. Hagg Farm
Hostel, Snake Road. Bamford, Sheffield. S30
2BJ

CAMPING—

Eric Byne Memorial Campsite,
Birchen Edge —
Grid Ref: SK 278723 Individual permits from
Mr. Smedley, Moorside Farm.
Tel. Baslow 2277
Parties of 4 or more, from Area Recreation
Office, Severn Trent Water Authority.
Meadow Lane, Nottingham Tel. Nottingham
(0602) 865007

BED AND BREAKFAST—

BASLOW—
Mrs J White, Rose-Hill Farm, Over-End,
Baslow. Nr. Bakewell Tel. Baslow 3280

Wheatsheaf Hotel,
Nether End, Baslow, Bakewell.
Tel. Baslow 2240

BAR BROOK AND THATCHED COTTAGE

17

GRITSTONE EDGE WALK—LOG

DATE.............................. TIME STARTED................ TIME COMPLETED...............

ROUTE POINT	MILE NO	TIME		COMMENTS
		ARR	DEP	
FAIRHOLMES	0			
WALKER'S CLOUGH	1			
GREEN SITCHES	2			
BACK TOR	3			
SALT CELLAR	4			
SHOOTING BUTTS	5			
MOSCAR	6			
A 57	7			
STANAGE END	8			
HIGH NEB	9			
STANAGE PLANTATION	10			
COWPER STONE	11			
BURBAGE ROCKS—NORTH	12			
BURBAGE ROCKS—SOUTH	13			
LONGSHAW	14			
GROUSE INN	15			
FROGGATT EDGE	16			
CURBAR EDGE	17			
BASLOW EDGE	18			
A621	19			
BIRCHENS EDGE	20			
CHATSWORTH EDGE	21			
BASLOW	22½			

GRITSTONE EDGE TRAIL PROFILE— 1,750 FEET OF ASCENT

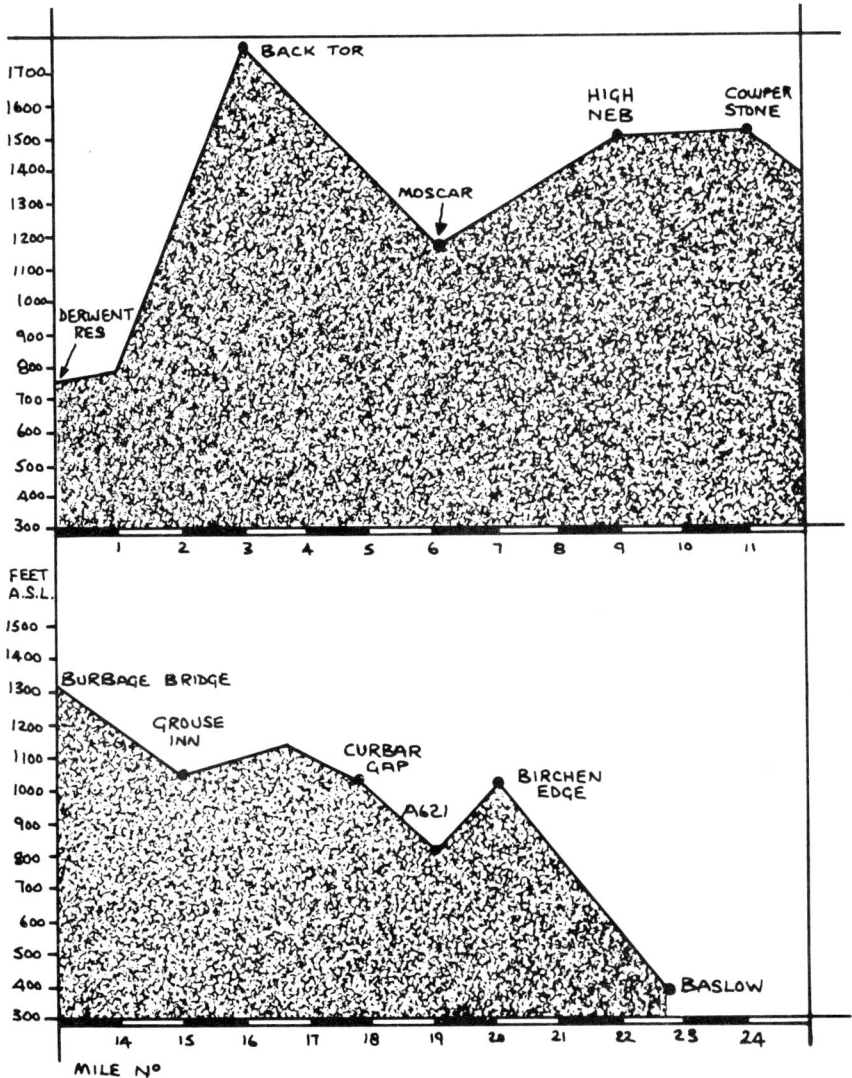

Upper chart labels:

- BACK TOR
- MOSCAR
- HIGH NEB
- COWPER STONE
- DERWENT RES

Vertical axis (upper): 1700, 1600, 1500, 1400, 1300, 1200, 1100, 1000, 900, 800, 700, 600, 500, 400, 300

Horizontal axis (upper): 1 2 3 4 5 6 7 8 9 10 11

FEET A.S.L.

Vertical axis (lower): 1500, 1400, 1300, 1200, 1100, 1000, 900, 800, 700, 600, 500, 400, 300

Lower chart labels:

- BURBAGE BRIDGE
- GROUSE INN
- CURBAR GAP
- A621
- BIRCHEN EDGE
- BASLOW

Horizontal axis (lower): 14 15 16 17 18 19 20 21 22 23 24

MILE N°

LIMESTONE DALE WALK—24 MILES

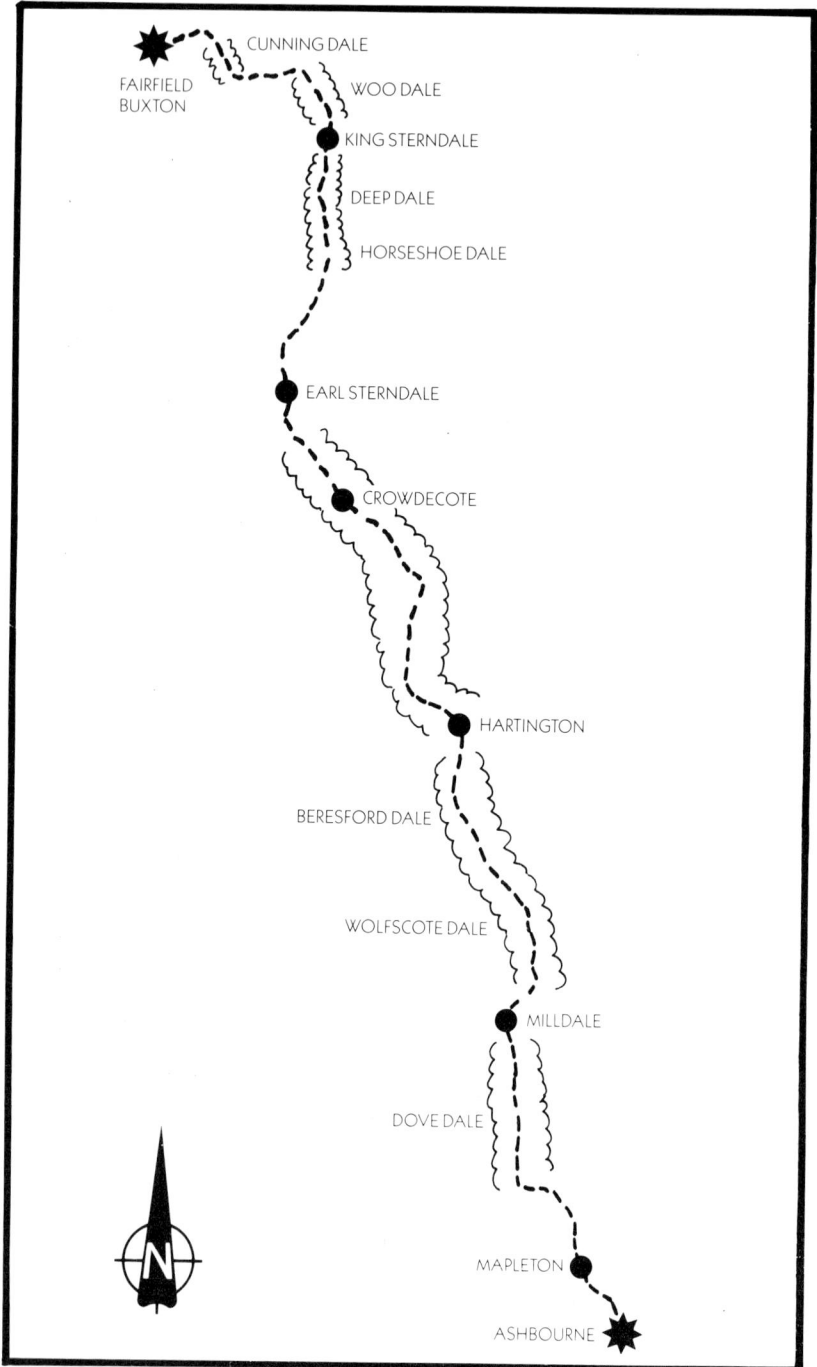

FAIRFIELD
BUXTON

CUNNING DALE

WOO DALE

KING STERNDALE

DEEP DALE

HORSESHOE DALE

EARL STERNDALE

CROWDECOTE

HARTINGTON

BERESFORD DALE

WOLFSCOTE DALE

MILLDALE

DOVE DALE

MAPLETON

ASHBOURNE

N

THE LIMESTONE DALE WALK—
24 MILES—allow 8/10 hours

ABOUT THE WALK—

Like the Gritstone Edge walk, this walk is another day job, with you being deposited at the start at Fairfield, on the outskirts of Buxton. Again it is a north to south route with only 1,400 feet of ascent on the way; much of the route is in the descent mode. Apart from a couple of inns, The Quiet Woman at Earl Sterndale and the Packhorse Inn at Crowdecote, there are no other facilities until Hartington, just over the half way point. Up to here the walking has been through a variety of quiet dales with no one to be seen.

The section from Hartington to the end of Dovedale is popular, and best avoided on Sundays and Bank Holidays in the summer months. Beyond is again quiet and solitude until you gain the Market Place and Cross in Ashbourne, where full facilities are to hand. I make no apology for including the Dovedale section for it is, despite the crowds and recent manicuring still a place of extraordinary beauty.

For those who complete the walk a special four colour embroidered badge on a grey (Limestone) background and a completion certificate is available from JNM Publications. A master record of all who walk the route is maintained by me.

The route is covered by the Ordnance Survey maps —
1:25,000 — Outdoor Leisure Map — The White Peak (West Sheet)
1:25,000 — Pathfinder Series — Sheet No SK 04/14 — Ashbourne and
the Churnet Valley.

BUXTON—at over 1,000 feet above sea level, it is the highest market town in England and Derbyshire's principal spa town. The healing waters were known to the Romans who named the place, Aquae Arnemetiae. Higher Buxton, where the Market Cross is, is the oldest part of the town. Lower Buxton around The Crescent is the new Buxton and much of it is the work of the 5th Duke of Devonshire in the late 18th century. The Crescent is said to have cost £120,000 and was designed by John Carr of York. The whole area is well worth exploring with St. John's Church, the Opera House, Pavilion and gardens and the Devonshire Hospital. Fairfield was a village in its own right but has become absorbed into Buxton. St. Peter's Church was founded in about 1260 AD. The present structure was largely rebuilt in 1839 with the transepts and chancel being added in 1902.

ASHBOURNE—full of historical buildings and well worth exploring, including the church and Church Street—the most complete 17th century street in Britain. Ashbourne is famous for its unique football game and locally made gingerbread men.

FAIRFIELD, BUXTON
TO EARL STERNDALE—7½ MILES

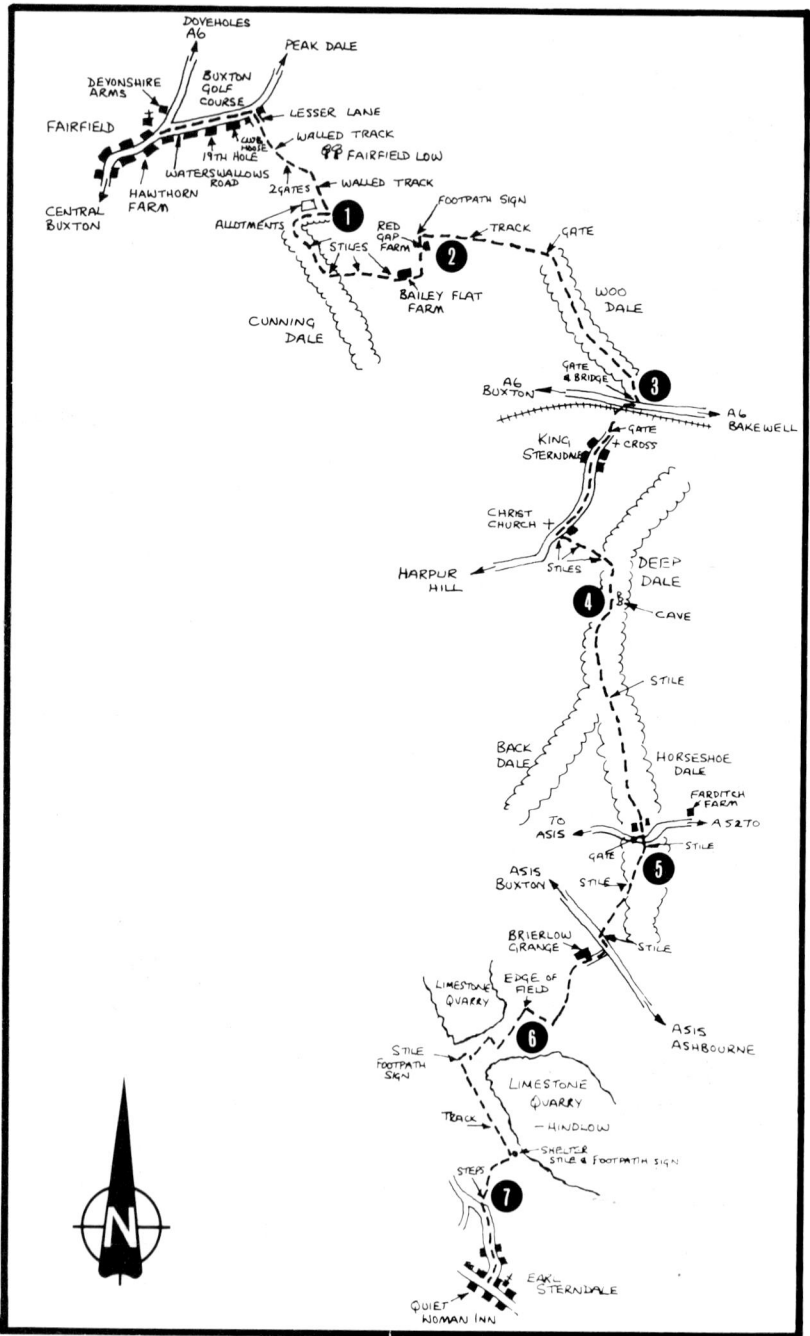

DOVEHOLES A6

PEAK DALE

DEVONSHIRE ARMS

BUXTON GOLF COURSE

FAIRFIELD

LESSER LANE

WALLED TRACK

CLUB HOUSE

19TH HOLE

FAIRFIELD LOW

WATERSWALLOWS ROAD

WALLED TRACK

HAWTHORN FARM

2 GATES

FOOTPATH SIGN

CENTRAL BUXTON

ALLOTMENTS

❶

RED GAP FARM

TRACK

GATE

STILES

❷

BAILEY FLAT FARM

WOO DALE

CUNNING DALE

GATE & BRIDGE

❸

A6 BUXTON

A6 BAKEWELL

GATE

CROSS

KING STERNDALE

CHRIST CHURCH

DEEP DALE

HARPUR HILL

STILES

❹

CAVE

STILE

BACK DALE

HORSESHOE DALE

FARDITCH FARM

TO ASIS

A 52 TO

STILE

GATE

❺

ASIS BUXTON

STILE

BRIERLOW GRANGE

STILE

LIMESTONE QUARRY

EDGE OF FIELD

ASIS ASHBOURNE

STILE FOOTPATH SIGN

❻

LIMESTONE QUARRY — HINDLOW

TRACK

SHELTER STILE & FOOTPATH SIGN

STEPS

❼

EARL STERNDALE

QUIET WOMAN INN

N

FAIRFIELD, BUXTON TO EARL STERNDALE—7½ MILES

ABOUT THE SECTION—

First you walk through two attractive dales before reaching the A6 road. A steep, but short ascent, brings you to the hamlet of King Sterndale. Here you descend into Deep Dale and walk up Horseshoe Dale to gain the A515 road. Crossed you continue ascending gently between limestone quarries before descending to Earl Sterndale and its views of the upper Doveland.

MAP—*1:25,000 Outdoor Leisure Map—The White Peak (West Sheet)*

WALKING INSTRUCTIONS—

Opposite Fairfield Church follow the Peak Dale road—Waterswallows Road—past the edge of the golf course on your left, club house on right and the 19th Hole Inn. After a ⅓ mile turn right into Lesser Lane and follow it past the houses into a walled track. Ahead can be seen your first dale—Cunning Dale—but to get there you walk round the three sides of a square. First pass through two gates beside a farm building and keep on the walled track as it swings right. At the end beneath a limestone slope turn right onto a path with a wall on your right as you pass near the allotment gardens on your right. Turn left into the dale and shortly afterwards bear left, angling up the dale side on a grass track which soon becomes a path. The path keeps close to the top of the dale with wall on your left. Pass through a stile and about 200 yards later in your third field on your left is a stone stile. Here leave the dale and follow the little used but well stiled path beside the wall to Bailey Flat Farm.

FAIRFIELD COTTAGES

23

Almost at the far end of the farm turn left past the cow sheds to a stile. Again the path is little used but you ascend the field to keep the wall on your right before descending to a stile beside a barn at Red Gap Farm. Turn left then right almost immediately, as footpath signposted, and walk along the grass track towards Woo Dale. After ¼ mile at a gate on your left leave the track and follow the grass track along the floor of Woo Dale. Keep on this for the next ¾ mile to the gate and bridge just before the A6 road. Ahead can be seen the steep ascent, with clear path and ladder stiles over the railway line. First turn right along the road for 20 yards before leaving it on your left and following the angled path to your right. Cross the line and continue ascending to a gate beside a walled track. Turn left and enter King Sterndale passing the base of a medieval Cross.

Continue heading southwards out of the village to the church on your right ¼ mile away. Almost opposite turn left over two stiles with a house on your immediate left. Cross the field to a stile and on across the next to a stile and the steep descent into Deep Dale—renowned for its rocky floor but one of the finest in the area. At the bottom turn right and pass the cave, and after a stile ¼ mile later bear left slightly to walk up Horseshoe Dale. At the top end pass through two gates between farm buildings and gain the A5270 road. Bear left to the other side of the road and behind the wooden fencing is the stile. The path is now ill-defined as you continue up Horseshoe Dale. Bear right and ascend the dale side to a stile beside a gate. Continue across the next field to a stile in the trees just below the A515 road.

Turn left and right along the road of Brierlow Grange. Continue ahead to the line of an old railway and turn left along it to a gate. Here turn right to another gate before turning right again and walking around the field edge, guided by path signs and wooden huts. At the stile follow the field edge beyond to reach the walled track where turn left. On either side of you is extensive quarrying. Follow the track for ½ mile passing concrete shelters. At the second turn right at the path sign and stile, and descend angling leftwards to some steps leading to the minor road. Turn left and descend into Earl Sterndale village to the Quiet Woman Inn.

KING STERNDALE CROSS

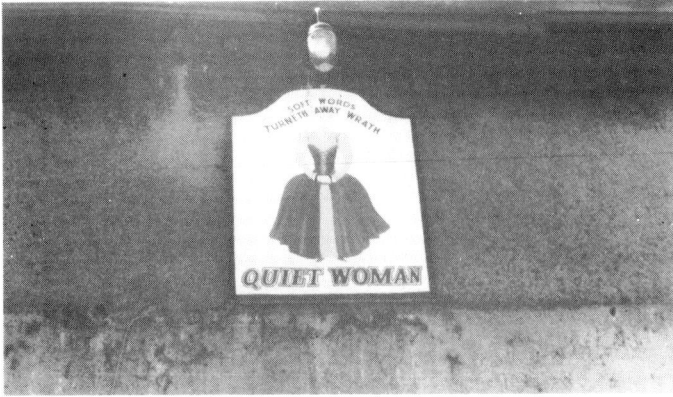

EARL STERNDALE—the inn—The Quiet Woman—depicts a headless woman, with the words, 'Soft words turneth away wrath.' Among the stories about the sign, one describes how a former landlady was a constant chatterbox. Eventually the locals could stand it no more and gave the landlord permission to decapitate her! Her tombstone is said to be a warning to other chatterboxes!

DEEP DALE

EARL STERNDALE
TO HARTINGTON—5 MILES

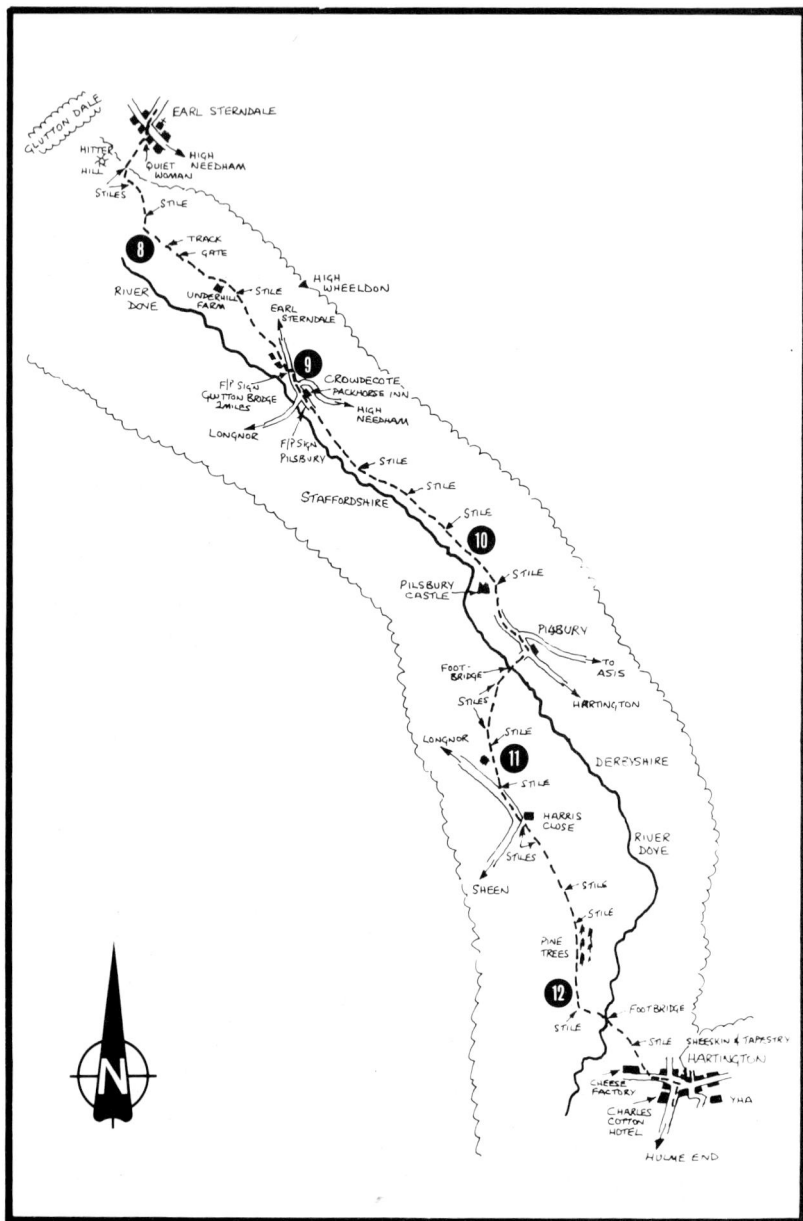

EARL STERNDALE TO HARTINGTON—5 MILES

ABOUT THE SECTION—

After viewing the reef knoll shapes of Parkhouse Hill and Chrome Hill you descend into the wide Dove valley and village of Crowdecote and the Packhorse Inn. The river Dove is the Derbyshire boundary and for the next two miles you keep in Derbyshire before crossing the river near Pilsbury into Staffordshire. Here you ascend to the valley edge, providing extensive views over the limestone country before descending to Hartington. The section makes a pleasant interlude from the narrow dales to wide river valleys, before following the last major dale system.

MAP—*1:25,000 Outdoor Leisure Map—The White Peak (West Sheet)*

WALKING INSTRUCTIONS—

Walk past the Quiet Woman Inn to your right to the path sign and turn left to ascend two stiled fields to the rim of the valley. Turn left after the second stile to another before descending towards your right to another stile. Here you descend to the gated track, beside a path sign and opposite Underhill. Turn left along the track and pass another solitary house to reach another walled track. Opposite is the stile and path to Crowdecote. At first it is a stiled path, but in the third field it develops into a track which takes you past the houses on your right to the minor road. Turn right to B5055 in Crowdecote village. Turn right then left past the Packhorse Inn and onto another track. Follow this past the houses on your left to a path sign—Pilsbury. Continue ahead on the track with the wall on your left to a stile. At the next one you emerge into the fields and follow a faint path across them heading for Pilsbury Castle. On your right can be seen the infant river Dove.

FOOTBRIDGE OVER RIVER DOVE, NEAR PILSBURY

27

The next two fields are well stiled and in the third, beneath the slopes of the castle, as path signed bear left up and around it to a stile and another track. Turn right along to the road at Pilsbury. Continue ahead along the road passing the farm buildings on your left. Pass through a gate and turn right down a track to a footbridge over the river Dove. Cross this and ascend the track for 75 yards to a stile on your left. Beyond angle leftwards as you ascend the field to a stile. Through this gain another and bear slightly right as you ascend to a stile near the valley rim with an abandoned farm building on your right. Continue ahead to the road, reached via a stile, and turn left.

Just before the first bend, 150 yards later, turn left at Harris Close and follow the path on the lefthand side on the wall. Keep the wall on your right for the next four fields where you leave it, passing right of two trees to gain another stile and the wall on your right. At the next stile you enter pine trees and at the other side after the stile you descend down the slope to a stile. Here the path bears left down the field to a footbridge over the river Dove. The path continues ahead before bearing right across the fields to Hartington Cheese factory. The path is well defined and stiled. Walk through the lefthand side of the factory to the road and turn left into central Hartington—car park and village pond.

HARTINGTON

MARKET PLACE, HARTINGTON

CROWDECOTE—small hamlet beside the river Dove on the Derbyshire/ Staffordshire boundary. Upstream are several large hills, which are former limestoe reef knolls—Hitter Hill, Parkhouse Hill and Chrome Hill. A former packhorse route crossed the Dove here, as the inn's name suggests. The hamlet's name stems from 'Crawdy Coat Bridge', which was originally wooden. A stone packhorse bridge was built here in 1709.

HARTINGTON—The Cheese factory is the only one left in Derbyshire today. Formerly Derbyshire was famous for cheese making, and in 1870 had England's first cheese factory at Longford. The Charles Cotton Hotel recalls the link with the River Dove and the fishing expertise of Izaak Walton and their famous book, 'The Compleat Angler'. The church dedicated to St. Giles has a plaque to Thomas Mellor, who died in 1822 aged 103. In the south transept is the only complete set of panels in this country of the Patriarchs of Israel.

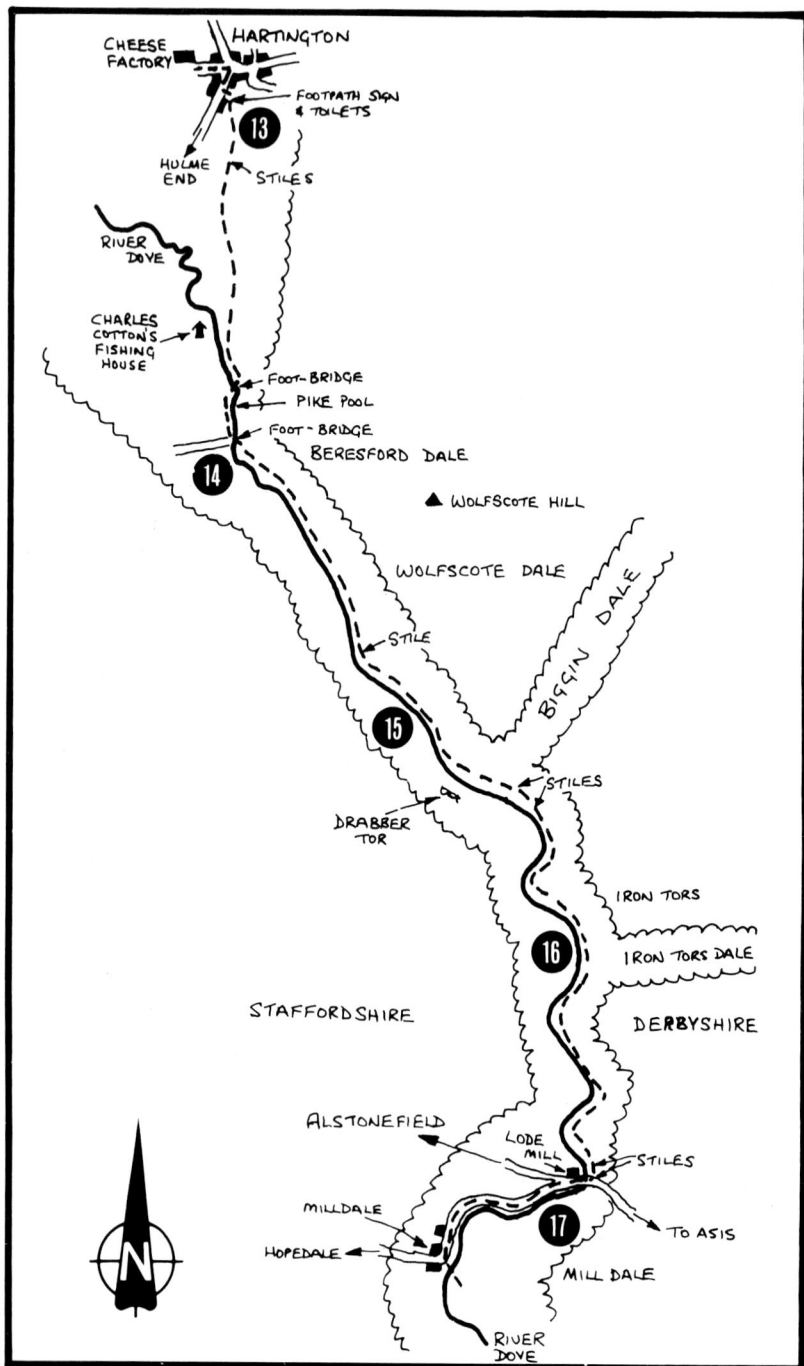

CHEESE FACTORY

HARTINGTON

FOOTPATH SIGN & TOILETS

13

HULME END

STILES

RIVER DOVE

CHARLES COTTON'S FISHING HOUSE

FOOT-BRIDGE

PIKE POOL

FOOT-BRIDGE

14

BERESFORD DALE

▲ WOLFSCOTE HILL

WOLFSCOTE DALE

BIGGIN DALE

STILE

15

STILES

DRABBER TOR

IRON TORS

16

IRON TORS DALE

STAFFORDSHIRE

DERBYSHIRE

ALSTONEFIELD

LODE MILL

STILES

MILLDALE

17

TO ASIS

HOPEDALE

MILL DALE

N

RIVER DOVE

HARTINGTON TO MILLDALE—4½ MILES

ABOUT THE SECTION—

Leaving Hartington you enter a series of limestone dales which are world renowned for their simple and dramatic beauty. The short narrow Beresford Dale before walking the length of Wolfscote dale with rocky and steep sides, while the river Dove grows in size pushing its way along over numerous weirs. The section is an apt curtain raiser to the next section.

MAP—*1:25,000 Outdoor Leisure Map — The White Peak (West Sheet)*

WALKING INSTRUCTIONS—

Bear right out of the Square in Hartington, passing the Charles Cotton Hotel on your right and shortly afterwards the Pottery and public toilets on your left. Here is the sign and well worn path, beside the toilets, into Beresford Dale. Turn left and follow it between the buildings before the path bears right to a walled track, crossed by stiles. The path can be seen stretching ahead down across the fields to woodland. Shortly after entering the trees you near the river before crossing it via a footbridge. Continue down through Beresford Dale to the road and footbridge on your left. Cross it and continue to your right across the field to a stile. Keep the river on your right and follow the well defined path beside it into Wolfscote Dale.

For the next three miles the river on your immediate right is your companion. After 1½ miles pass the entrance to Biggin Dale on your left, with a shallow cave just ahead. Another mile brings you past Iron Tors Dale also on your left, and ¾ mile later reach the minor road at Lode Mill. Cross the bridge and turn left and follow it to Milldale.

WOLFSCOTE DALE

31

MILLDALE TO DOVEDALE STEPPING STONES—2½ MILES

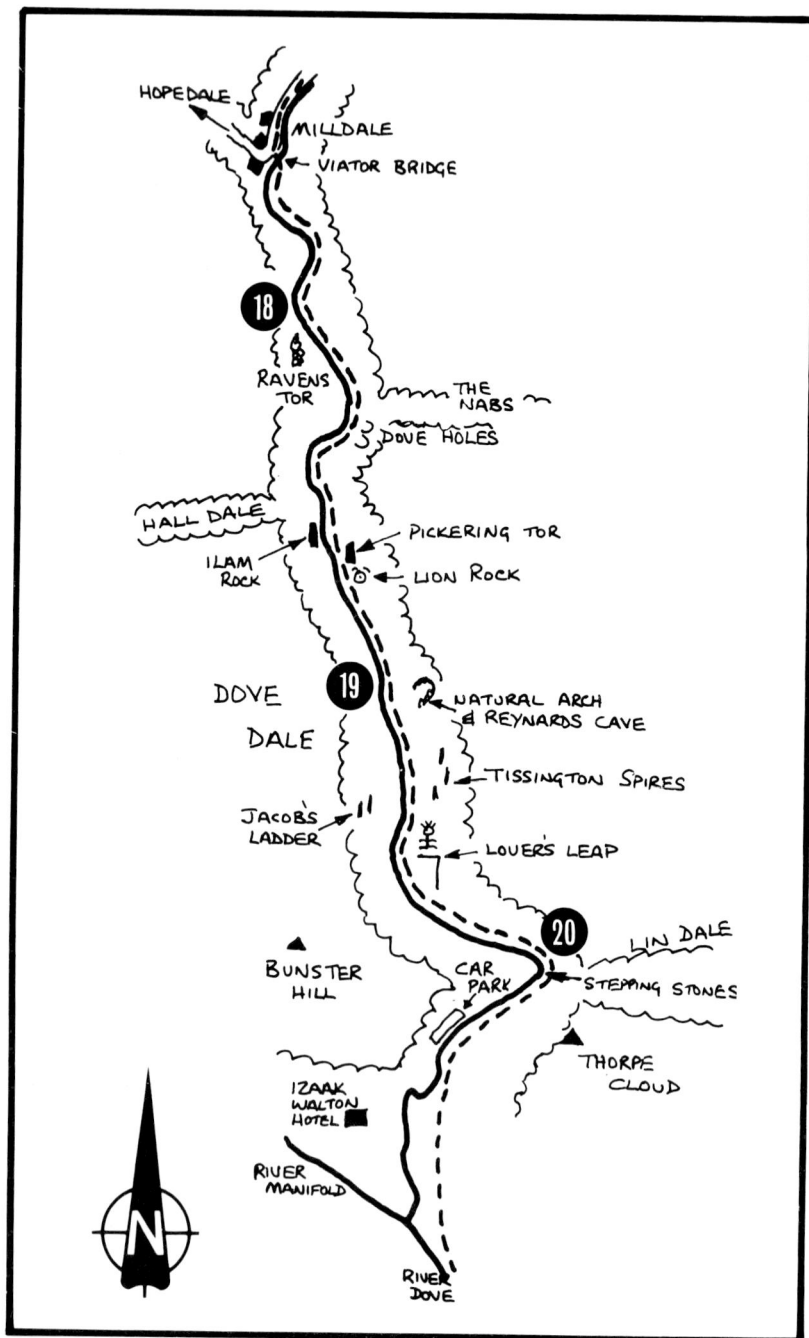

HOPEDALE

MILLDALE

VIATOR BRIDGE

18

RAVENS TOR

THE NABS

DOVE HOLES

HALL DALE

PICKERING TOR

ILAM ROCK

LION ROCK

DOVE DALE

19

NATURAL ARCH & REYNARDS CAVE

TISSINGTON SPIRES

JACOB'S LADDER

LOVER'S LEAP

20

LIN DALE

BUNSTER HILL

CAR PARK

STEPPING STONES

THORPE CLOUD

IZAAK WALTON HOTEL

RIVER MANIFOLD

N

RIVER DOVE

MILLDALE TO DOVEDALE
STEPPING STONES—2½ MILES

ABOUT THE SECTION—

Despite Dovedale's popularity the dale is a magnificent walk, even with tired legs after a walk of about 20 miles walk. The limestone rock scenery is impressive with Ravens Tor, Dove Holes, Ilam Rock, Pickering Tor, Reynard Cave and natural arch, numerous rock spires and Lover's Leap vantage point. The path is manicured in places with fencing, broadwalks and steps. Rock climbers abound, and on my final run through for the book in the space of five minutes I saw a fisherman catch a fish and two separate climbers fall twenty feet on opposite sides of the dale!

MAP—*1:25,000 Outdoor Leisure Map—The White Peak (West Sheet)*

WALKING INSTRUCTIONS—

Cross Viator's Bridge opposite the toilets and shop in Milldale and enter Dovedale. The path is well used, and for the next three miles the river keeps you company on your right, as you pass the various rock formations and shapes along the way. Continue to the stepping stones, the end of this stage, beneath the slopes of Thorpe Cloud.

NATURAL ARCH, DOVEDALE

33

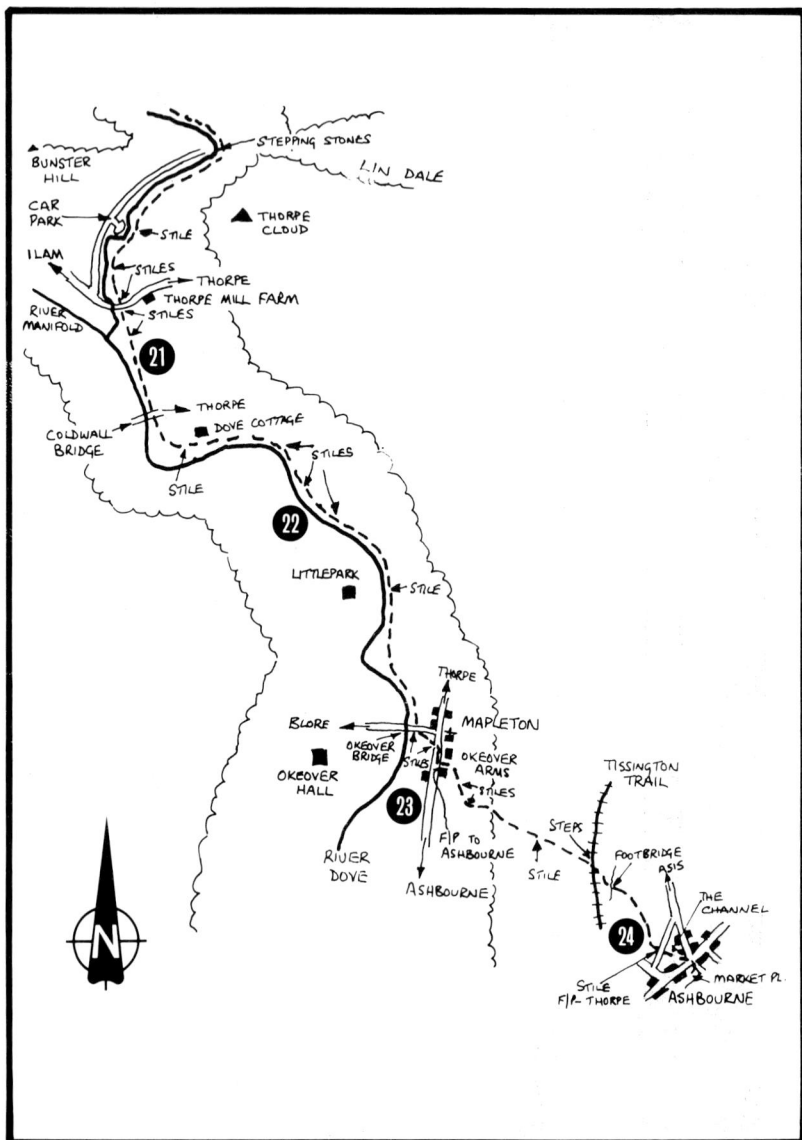

COLDWALL BRIDGE—built in 1726 and part of an old coaching road. On the Thorpe side can be seen a milestone—'Cheadle (Staffordshire) 11 miles.'

MAPLETON—18th century aisle-less church. Okeover Hall dates from the 17th century.

DOVEDALE STEPPING STONES TO ASHBOURNE—4½ MILES

ABOUT THE SECTION—

After crossing the Ilam—Thorpe road, in a little over ½ mile you are back into quiet country. The path is little used but is well stiled and simple to follow, with the river Dove as your companion to Mapleton. Here you leave it and—sorry—you have two ascents to do to gain Ashbourne. Bit cruel at the end of the walk but it wouldn't a challenge otherwise! To reach Ashbourne Market Place you descend The Channel which should be done at a jogging pace. In the Market Place the Cross serves as your finishing post!

MAPS—*1:25,000 Outdoor Leisure Map—The White Peak (West Sheet)—1:25,000 Pathfinder Series— Sheet No SK 04/14—Ashbourne and the Churnet Valley.*

WALKING INSTRUCTIONS—

Don't cross the stepping stones, simply continue ahead on the path beside the river at the base of Thorpe Cloud. Once past the footbridge to the car park the path becomes faint but is well stiled as you keep near the river on your right. After ¼ mile reach the minor road. Cross it to your left to the next stile. You leave the riverside now for the next two fields, but the stiles guide you. A little over ½ mile later reach Coldwall Bridge. Cross over to the track and follow it briefly before swinging left to a stile on your right, passing in front of Dove Cottage (1867). Signs indicate the route. For the next 1 ½ miles you keep the river Dove close by on the right and the path is well stiled. Gain Okeover Bridge and cross to the next stile and path sign. Turn left across the field to enter Mapleton village opposite the Okeover Arms.

Cross the road and just ahead on your left is the fenced path, signposted—Ashbourne. Pass between the houses to the stile and turn right ascending to the next stile. Pass through another and, at the end of the wall on your left, turn left and ascend passing through more stiles. Cross the crest of the hill to another stile and begin the descent to the Tissington Trail. Ascend the steps up to the trail and cross over to more steps and path which curves to your right and down to the footbridge over Bentley Brook. Continue ahead and begin ascending a short distance before turning right and following the path across the field, ascending to your right to the houses and stile. Ascend this and gain the road beside the footpath sign—Thorpe. Cross over and descend The Channel into Ashbourne Market Place. Don't forget to touch the Cross— now you can relax, it is all over!

PLACE	TELEPHONE	TOILETS	CAR PARK	POST OFFICE	SHOP	RESTAURANT	INN	CAMPING	YHA	B&B
BUXTON	●	●	●	●	●	●	●	●	●	●
KING STERNDALE	●									●
BRIERLEY GRANGE										●
EARL STERNDALE	●					●				
CROWDECOTE	●					●				●
HARTINGTON	●	●	●	●	●	●	●	●	●	●
MILLDALE	●	●	●		●					
END OF DOVEDALE	●	●	●				●		●	●
MAPLETON	●			●	●		●			
ASHBOURNE	●	●	●	●	●	●	●	●		●

There are a variety of amenities actually on the route, especially at Hartington. Both Buxton and Ashbourne have every amenity.

INNS— actually passed on the route

Devonshire Arms, Buxton
The 19th Hole, Buxton
The Quiet Woman, Earl Sterndale
The Packhorse Inn, Crowdecote
Devonshire Arms, Hartington
The Charles Cotton Hotel, Hartington
Izaak Walton Hotel, just off the route at the end
of Dovedale
Okeover Arms, Mapleton
The George & Dragon Hotel, Ashbourne
The White Swan, Ashbourne

BED AND BREAKFAST—

Buxton—	Hawthorn Farm Guest House, Fairfield Road, Buxton. Tel. Buxton 3230 There are numerous others in central Buxton.
Crowdecote—	Packhorse Inn, Crowdecote, Buxton Tel. Longnor 210
Hartington—	Mrs B. Blackburn, Bank House, Market Place, Hartington. Tel. Hartington (029884) 465
Ashbourne—	Compton Guest House, Compton, Ashbourne. Tel. Ashbourne 43100
	Mrs J. Byworth, The Hollies, 73, The Green Road, Ashbourne. Tel. Ashbourne 42514

YOUTH HOSTELS

Buxton—	Sherbrook Lodge, Harpur Hill Road, Buxton, Derbyshire. Tel. Buxton 2287
Hartington—	Hartington Hall, Hartington, Buxton, Derbys. Tel. Hartington 463
Ilam—	1 mile off route. Ilam Hall, Ashbourne, Derbyshire. Tel. Thorpe Cloud 212

CAMPING

Buxton—	J.G.Turner, The Punch Bowl, Manchester Road. G.R. SK 050740 Tel. Buxton 4321
Hartington—	W.R.Jackson, Barracks Farm, Beresford Dale G.R. SK 124587 Tel. Hartington 261
Ashbourne—	A.C.Palmer, Callow Top Caravan Site. G.R. SK 174476 Tel. Ashbourne 43726

MAPLETON

LIMESTONE DALE WALK—LOG

DATE .... TIME STARTED .... TIME COMPLETED ....

ROUTE POINT	MILE NO	TIME		COMMENTS
		ARR	DEP	
FAIRFIELD, BUXTON	0			
CUNNING DALE	1			
WOO DALE	2½			
A6	3			
KING STERNDALE	3½			
DEEP DALE	4			
HORSESHOE DALE	4½			
A5270	5			
A515	5½			
QUARRIES	6½			
EARL STERNDALE	7½			
CROWDECOTE	9			
PILSBURY	10½			
HARRIS CLOSE	11¼			
HARTINGTON	13			
BERESFORD DALE	13½			
WOLFSCOTE DALE	15			
LODE MILL	17			
MILLDALE	17½			
DOVE HOLES	18½			
REYNARDS CAVE	19			
STEPPING STONES	20			
ILAM ROAD	21			
COLDWALL BRIDGE	21¼			
MAPLETON	23			
TISSINGTON TRAIL	23¾			
ASHBOURNE	24¼			

LIMESTONE DALE TRAIL PROFILE— 1,400 FEET OF ASCENT

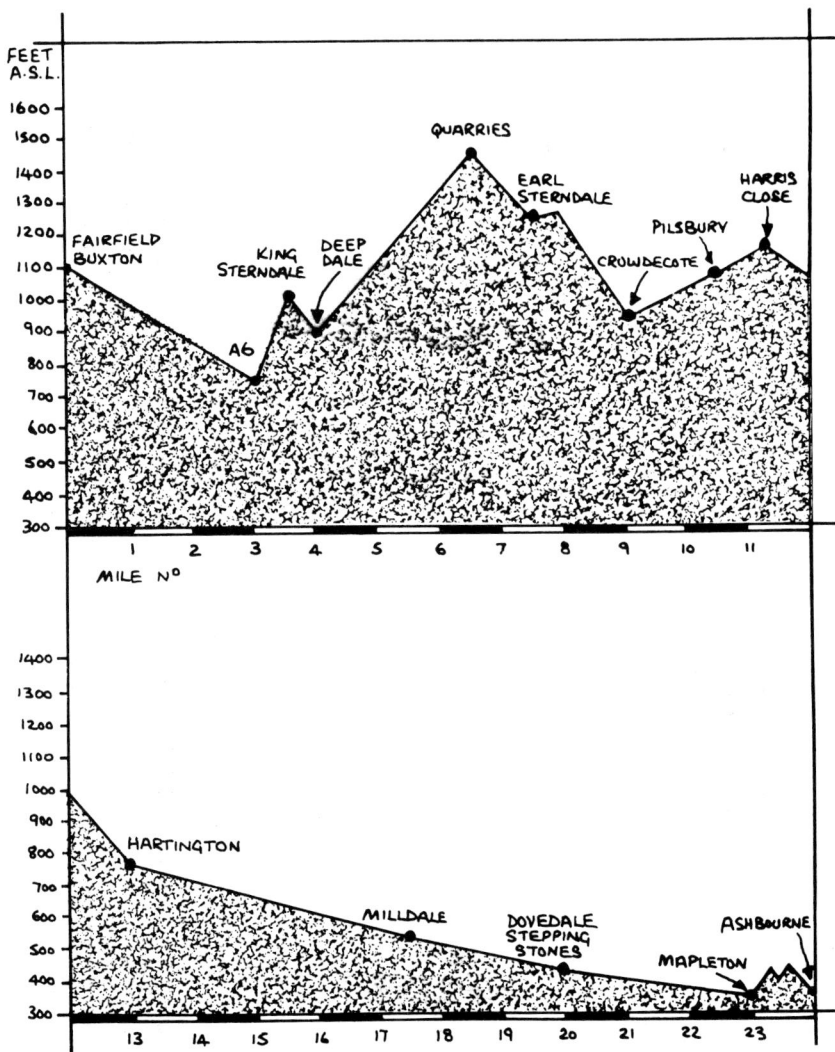

FEET
A.S.L.

1600
1500
1400
1300
1200
1100
1000
900
800
700
600
500
400
300

QUARRIES

EARL
STERNDALE

HARRIS
CLOSE

PILSBURY

FAIRFIELD
BUXTON

KING
STERNDALE

DEEP
DALE

CROWDECOTE

A6

1 2 3 4 5 6 7 8 9 10 11

MILE N°

1400
1300
1200
1100
1000
900
800
700
600
500
400
300

HARTINGTON

MILLDALE

DOVEDALE
STEPPING
STONES

ASHBOURNE

MAPLETON

13 14 15 16 17 18 19 20 21 22 23

BIRD AND FLOWER CHECKLIST

This is a random checklist of some of the more common flowers and birds to be seen on the walks. Between the two walks you cross a wide variety of terrain—moorland, gritstone country, coniferous forests and limestone dales—and will see a diverse range of species.

BIRDS

MOORLAND

Red Grouse
Meadow Pipit
Golden Plover
Dunlin
Skylark

Ring Ouzel
Wheatear
Curlew
Twite

GRITSTONE COUNTRY

Tree-creeper
Great Spotted Woodpecker
Whinchat
Common Sandpiper
Grey Heron
Starling
Chaffinch
Bullfinch
Crow
Wren
Blue Tit
Great Tit
Robin
Long Tailed Tit
Greenfinch

Skylark
Coot
Rook
Pheasant
Wood
Pigeon
Song Thrush
Magpie
Linnet
Moorhen
Blackbird
Cuckoo
Black Headed Gull
Mistle Thrush
House Sparrow

LIMESTONE COUNTRY

Tree-Creeper
Nuthatch
Wheatear
Curlew
Kingfisher
Dipper
Grey Wagtail
Mallard
Tufted Duck

Little Owl
Robin
Redstart
Sedge Warbler
Redpoll
Swallow
Pied Wagtail
Wren
Blue Tit

Great Tit
Moorhen
Coot
Blackbird
Raven
Lapwing
Fieldfare

Lesser Black Backed Gull
Marsh Tits
Bullfinch
Hawfinch
Wood Pigeon
Whitethroat
Yellowhammer

FLOWERS

MOORLAND

Ling
Cowberry
Crowberry
Butterwort
Sphagnum
Moss
Maidenhair
Spleenwort

Fern
Bilberry
Cranberry
Bog
Asphodel
Round-leaved Sundew
Cotton Grass

GRITSTONE COUNTRY

Bilberry
Wood Sorrel
Bluebell
Hard Fern
Wavy Hair Grass
Ling
Eyebright
Devil's Bit Scabious
Sheep's Sorrel
Tormentil
Sheep's Fescue
Common Bent
Mat Grass
Purple Moor-Grass
Heath Bedstraw

Red Campion
Lesser Celandine
Poppy
Clover
Snowberry
Sneezewort
Marsh Thistle
Meadowsweet
Policemen's Helmet
Gorse
Periwinkle
Marsh Marigold
Foxglove
Honesty
Yellow Loosestrife

LIMESTONE COUNTRY

Meadow Cranesbill
Dog's Mercury
Ramsons
Wood Anemone
Arum
Butterbur
Wood Sorrel
Herb Robert
Ground Ivy
Wood Forget-Me-Not
Crosswort
Lesser Meadow Rue
Bloody Cranesbill
Mossy Saxifrage
Sheep's Fescue
Slender Bedstraw
Devil's Bit
Scabious Milkwort
Carline Thistle
Cowslip
Early Purple Orchid
Jacob's Ladder
Mountain Pansies
Scurvygrass
Male Fern
Coltsfoot
Rosebay Willow-herb
Ragged Robin
Lady's Smock
Knapweed
Gorse
Blackthorn
Marsh Marigold
Ox-Eye Daisy
Bluebell
Primrose
Lilly of the Valley
Mountain Melick

Wood Sage
Greater Burnet Saxifrage
Globe Flower
Nettle-leaved Bell Flower
Musk Thistle
Marjoram
Thyme
Harebell
Rough Hawkbit
Small Scabious
Kidney Vetch
Rock Rose
Eyebright
Clustered Bell Flower
Hawkweed Oxtongue
Grass of Parnassus
Birdsfoot Trefoil
Germander Speedwell
Monkey Flower
Hart's Tongue Fern
Twayblade
White Dead Nettle
Yellow Archangel
Meadow Buttercup
Great Hairy Willow-herb
Watercress
Red Campion
Lesser Celandine
Foxglove
Clover
Yellow Stonecrop
Goatsbeard
Rattle
Limestone Fern
Stitchwort
Bugle
Dog Rose
Tufted Vetch

EQUIPMENT NOTES—some personal thoughts

BOOTS—preferably with a leather upper, of medium weight, with a vibram sole. I always add a foam cushioned insole to help cushion the base of my feet.

SOCKS—I generally wear two thick pairs as this helps to minimise blisters. The inner pair of loop stitch variety and approximately 80% wool. The outer a thick rib pair of approximately 80% wool.

WATERPROOFS—for general walking I wear a T shirt or shirt with a cotton wind jacket on top. You generate heat as you walk and I prefer to layer my clothes to avoid getting too hot. Depending on the season will dictate how many layers you wear. In soft rain I just use my wind jacket for I know it quickly dries out. In heavy downpours I slip on a neoprene lined cagoule, and although hot and clammy it does keep me reasonably dry. Only in extreme conditions will I don overtrousers, much preferring to get wet and feel comfortable.

FOOD—as I walk I carry bars of chocolate, for they provide instant energy and are light to carry. In winter a flask of hot coffee is welcome. I never carry water and find no hardship from doing so, but this is a personal matter. From experience I find the more I drink the more I want. You should always carry some extra food such as Kendal Mint Cake for emergencies.

RUCKSACK—for day walking I use a climbing rucksac of about 40 litre capacity and although excess space it does mean that the sac is well padded and with a shoulder strap. Inside apart from the basics for the day I carry gloves, balaclava, spare pullover and a pair of socks.

MAP & COMPASS—when I am walking I always have the relevant map—usually 1:25,000 scale—open in my hand. This enables me to constantly check that I am walking the right way. In case of bad weather I carry a Silva type compass, which once mastered gives you complete confidence in thick cloud or mist.

REMEMBER AND OBSERVE
THE COUNTRY CODE

ENJOY THE COUNTRYSIDE AND RESPECT ITS LIFE AND WORK.

GUARD AGAINST ALL RISK OF FIRE.

FASTEN ALL GATES.

KEEP YOUR DOGS UNDER CLOSE CONTROL.

KEEP TO PUBLIC PATHS ACROSS FARMLAND.

USE GATES AND STILES TO CROSS FENCES, HEDGES AND WALLS.

LEAVE LIVESTOCK, CROPS AND MACHINERY ALONE.

TAKE YOUR LITTER HOME—PACK IT IN, PACK IT OUT.

HELP TO KEEP ALL WATER CLEAN.

PROTECT WILDLIFE, PLANTS AND TREES.

TAKE SPECIAL CARE ON COUNTRY ROADS.

MAKE NO UNNECESSARY NOISE.

ABOUT THE WALKS –

Whilst every care is taken detailing and describing the walks in this book, it should be bourne in mind that the countryside changes by the seasons and the work of man. I have described the walks to the best of my ability detailing what I have found on the walk in the way of stiles and signs. Obviously with the passage of time stiles become broken or replaced by a ladder stile or even a small gate. Signs too have a habit of being broken or pushed over. All the routes follow rights of way and only on rare occasions will you have to overcome obstacle in its path, such as a barbed wire fence or electric fence.

The seasons bring occasional problems whilst out walking which should also be bourne in mind. In the height of summer paths become overgrown and you will have to fight your way through in a few places. In low lying areas the fields are full of crops and although the pathline goes straight across it may be more practical to walk round the field edge to get to the next stile or gate. In summer the ground is generally dry but in autumn and winter, especially because of our climate, the surface can be decidedly wet and slippery; sometimes even glutonous mud!

These comments are part of countryside walking which help to make your walk more interesting or briefly frustrating. Standing in a farmyard upto your ankles in mud might not be funny at the time but upon reflection was one of the highlights of the walk!

OTHER BOOKS BY JOHN N. MERRILL PUBLISHED BY JNM PUBLICATIONS

DAY WALK GUIDES –

SHORT CIRCULAR WALKS IN THE PEAK DISTRICT
LONG CIRCULAR WALKS IN THE PEAK DISTRICT
CIRCULAR WALKS IN WESTERN PEAKLAND
SHORT CIRCULAR WALKS IN THE STAFFORDSHIRE MOORLANDS
PEAK DISTRICT TOWN WALKS
SHORT CIRCULAR WALKS AROUND MATLOCK
SHORT CIRCULAR WALKS IN THE DUKERIES
SHORT CIRCULAR WALKS IN SOUTH YORKSHIRE
SHORT CIRCULAR WALKS AROUND DERBY
SHORT CIRCULAR WALKS AROUND BUXTON
SHORT CIRCULAR WALKS AROUND NOTTINGHAMSHIRE
SHORT CIRCULAR WALKS ON THE NORTHERN MOORS
40 SHORT CIRCULAR PEAK DISTRICT WALKS
SHORT CIRCULAR WALKS IN THE HOPE VALLEY

INSTRUCTION & RECORD –

HIKE TO BE FIT..STROLLING WITH JOHN
THE JOHN MERRILL WALK RECORD BOOK

CANAL WALK GUIDES –

VOL ONE — DERBYSHIRE AND NOTTINGHAMSHIRE
VOL TWO — CHESHIRE AND STAFFORDSHIRE
VOL THREE — STAFFORDSHIRE
VOL FOUR — THE CHESHIRE RING

DAY CHALLENGE WALKS –

JOHN MERRILL'S PEAK DISTRICT CHALLENGE WALK
JOHN MERRILL'S YORKSHIRE DALES CHALLENGE WALK
JOHN MERRILL'S NORTH YORKSHIRE MOORS CHALLENGE WALK
PEAK DISTRICT END TO END WALKS
THE LITTLE JOHN CHALLENGE WALK
JOHN MERRILL'S LAKELAND CHALLENGE WALK
JOHN MERRILL'S STAFFORDSHIRE MOORLAND CHALLENGE WALK
JOHN MERRILL'S DARK PEAK CHALLENGE WALK

MULTIPLE DAY WALKS –

THE RIVERS' WAY
PEAK DISTRICT HIGH LEVEL ROUTE
PEAK DISTRICT MARATHONS
THE LIMEY WAY
THE PEAKLAND WAY

COAST WALKS –

ISLE OF WIGHT COAST WALK
PEMBROKESHIRE COAST PATH
THE CLEVELAND WAY

HISTORICAL GUIDES –

DERBYSHIRE INNS
HALLS AND CASTLES OF THE PEAK DISTRICT & DERBYSHIRE
TOURING THE PEAK DISTRICT AND DERBYSHIRE BY CAR
DERBYSHIRE FOLKLORE
LOST INDUSTRIES OF DERBYSHIRE
PUNISHMENT IN DERBYSHIRE
CUSTOMS OF THE PEAK DISTRICT AND DERBYSHIRE
WINSTER — A VISITOR'S GUIDE
ARKWRIGHT OF CROMFORD
TALES FROM THE MINES by GEOFFREY CARR
PEAK DISTRICT PLACE NAMES by MARTIN SPRAY

JOHN'S MARATHON WALKS –

TURN RIGHT AT LAND'S END
WITH MUSTARD ON MY BACK
TURN RIGHT AT DEATH VALLEY
EMERALD COAST WALK

COLOUR GUIDES –

THE PEAK DISTRICT .... Something to remember her by.

SKETCH BOOKS — by John Creber

NORTH STAFFORDSHIRE SKETCHBOOK

PEAK END TO END

Badges are brown cloth for the Gritstone Edge Walk and grey cloth for the Limestone Dale Walk. Both have figure embroidered in four colours and measure 3" wide×3½" high.

*************** YOU MAY PHOTOCOPY THIS FORM ************

BADGE ORDER FORM

Gritstone Edge Walk/Limestone Dale Walk

Date completed...

Time ....

Name..

Address ....

Price: £   **Badges & Certificates are**   npletion certificate.
From: J   **£3.00 each from –**   shire. DE4 2DQ
Tel: Wir   *Happy Walking International Ltd.,*
Unit 1, Molyneux Business Park,
Whitworth Road, Darley Dale,
THE JC   **Matlock, Derbyshire. DE4 2HJ**   ıble to anyone who
walks t   **Tel/Fax 01629 - 735911**   ın Merrill's challenge
walks.   se who have walked
the routes—are circular, embroidered in four colours on a black
cloth. Price £1.75 each.

47